Space

Earth

Charlotte Guillain

Heinemann Library
Chicago, Illinois

Editorial: Rebecca Rissman, Charlotte Guillain, and Siân Smith
Picture research: Tracy Cummins and Heather Mauldin
Designed by Joanna Hinton-Malivoire
Printed and bound by South China Printing Company Limited

13 12 11 10 09
10 9 8 7 6 5 4 3 2 1

ISBN-13: 978-1-4329-2745-5 (hc)
ISBN-13: 978-1-4329-2752-3 (pb)

Library of Congress Cataloging-in-Publication Data

Guillain, Charlotte.
 Earth / Charlotte Guillain.
    p. cm. -- (Space)
 Includes bibliographical references and index.
 ISBN 978-1-4329-2745-5 (hc) -- ISBN 978-1-4329-2752-3 (pb)
 1. Earth--Juvenile literature. 2. Solar system--Juvenile literature. I. Title.
 QB631.4.G85 2008
 525--dc22
                                       2008049206

Acknowledgments
The author and publisher are grateful to the following for permission to reproduce copyright material:
Getty Images pp. **7** (©Philippe Bourseiller), **8** (©Peter Cade), **10** (©Hedgehog House /Colin Monteath), **17, 23b** (©Stocktrek Images); Jupiter Images pp.**9** (©The Stocktrek Corp), **14** (©Jean-Louis Bellurget), **22** (©The Stocktrek Corp); NASA p. **6** (©Goddard Space Flight Center (NASA-GSFC); Photo Researchers Inc p.**15** (©Planetary Visions Ltd); Photolibrary p.**4** (©Albert Klein); Shutterstock pp.**5** (©Dabobabo), **11** (©Maga), **16** (©Patrick Hermans), **18** (©Andrea Danti), **20** (©DJM-photo), **23c** (©Maga).

Front cover photograph reproduced with permission of NASA (©Goddard Space Flight Center (NASA-GSFC)). Back cover photograph reproduced with permission of Jupiter Images (©The Stocktrek Corp).

Every effort has been made to contact copyright holders of any material reproduced in this book. Any omissions will be rectified in subsequent printings if notice is given to the publisher.

Contents

Planets

Planets are in space.

Space is up above the sky.

Earth

Earth is a planet.

Earth is a planet made of rock.

Most of Earth is covered in water.

The water makes Earth look blue.

There are living things on Earth.

Living things need the Sun to live.

Equator

The middle of Earth gets a lot of sunlight all year. The middle of Earth is warm.

12

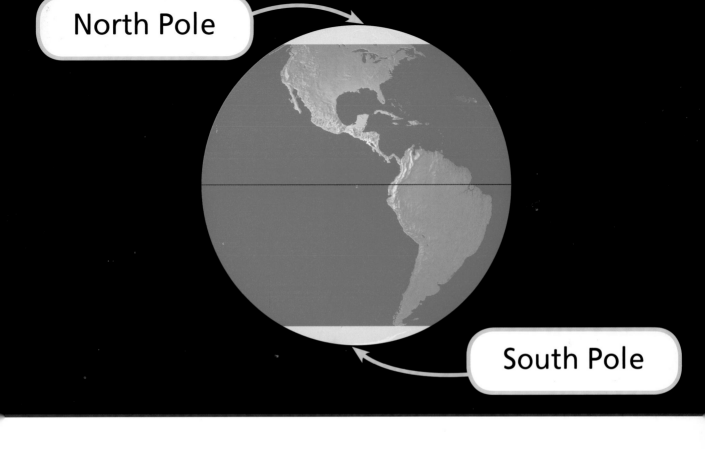

North Pole

South Pole

The North and South Poles do not get much sunlight.

People live on Earth.

You can see where people live
from space.

The Solar System

There are eight planets in the Solar System.

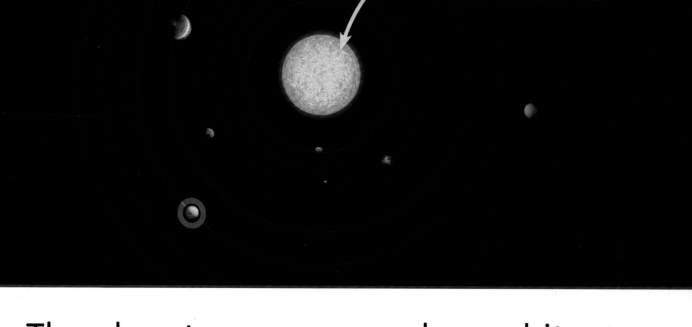

the Sun

The planets move around, or orbit, the Sun.

the Sun

Earth

Earth is quite close to the Sun.

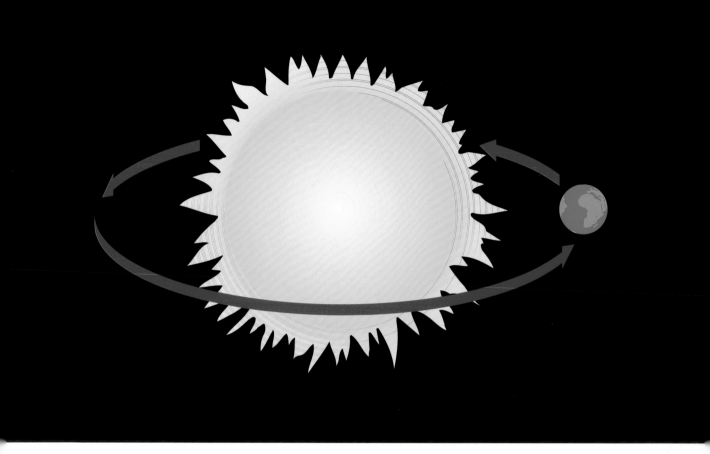

Earth takes one year to orbit the Sun.

The Moon

Earth has a moon.

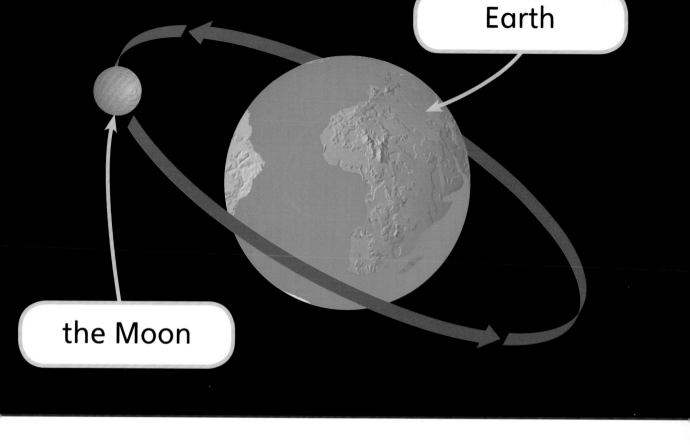

Earth

the Moon

The Moon orbits Earth.

Can You Remember?

What makes the Earth look blue?

22

Answer on p. 24

Picture Glossary

 **orbit** move around

 **Solar System** the name for the Sun and the eight planets that move around it

 **Sun** the star closest to Earth. The Sun gives us light and heat.

Index

Answer to question on p. 22: Water makes the Earth look blue.

Note to Parents and Teachers

Before reading

Show children a globe and explain that it represents the Earth. Tell them that if they were in space Earth would look like the globe, a round turning ball. Point out the oceans and tell them that most of the Earth is covered in water. When astronauts sent back pictures of Earth from space it was easy to see the areas of land and water. Find the country where they live.

After reading

• Ask the children to sit in a circle. Give each of them the name of a space vehicle, such as "flying saucer," "rocket," "moon buggy," and "space shuttle." Call out all "space shuttles." Explain that they are going to orbit Earth by moving around the outside of the circle. On the instruction "Back to Earth," they should return their places and sit down. Repeat the command with other space vehicles.